T0304431

sweet nothing

Sweet Nothing

PROSE, POEMS, & PLAYS

KAZIM ALI

Spout Press
Minneapolis, MN

Sweet Nothing
Kazim Ali

ISBN 978-0-9659443-2-8

cover art by Kazim Ali

Spout Press is a member of CLMP and is distributed to the trade
by Small Press Distribution, Berkeley, CA
(www.spdbooks.org)

Published by
Spout Press
P.O. Box 581067
Minneapolis, MN 55458-1067

The story is always somewhere else. I imagine a book that pretends to tell an official story. In the margins there is another story. It is incidental, it has little bearing on the official story, but it is where the real story is.

—Kristjana Gunnars

contents

prose

plays

poems

prose

Sweet Nothing

When people ask me, "What are you up to?" normally I say, "Nothing," followed by the actual something I'm up to. It's as if the fundamental "nothing" has to be acknowledged first: what follows is the description of the existential "nothing" I happen at the moment to be up to, which in the case of this morning is driving around from one drugstore to another trying to figure out where to get a rapid COVID test. I'm vaccinated, but the people I was with last night texted me to let me know that they had been with a group the day before in which someone had just tested positive.

I remember doing math like this about probabilities of transmission: for example, I could tell you that the chances of a negative top contracting HIV from unprotected sex with a positive bottom are something like 1 in 1,000. The numbers seem impossibly low, but at least at one point in the past they were documented by medical science.

At any rate, I was driving through my old neighborhood, the one we lived in when I was growing up. It had been nearly thirty-five years but things, including the trees, looked surprisingly the same. I knew it couldn't be true of the trees; what's more likely is that they grew large, were cut down, new trees were planted and they grew again. I'm generations removed from the boy who lived here.

I didn't really feel any sense of nostalgia or immediacy of sensation until I passed the house on the corner where Mark lived. He was a grade older than me and (I thought) very handsome, though all the other kids used to bully him and call him "gay" on the bus ride home. He never responded to them, and they somehow were so fixated on him that they never noticed me. I don't remember when Mark and I became friends but I do remember that besides endless games of Dungeons and Dragons (me as the Dungeon Master and him as the only player), our favorite activity was wrestling with each other in the basement of our house. I don't remember ever going to his house but I do remember I pinned him as often as he pinned me even though he was a year older, and stronger.

The warmth of the memory of his weight on top of me suddenly radiated through me and my ears started buzzing. I thought of Bob, who lived in the house next to ours whose father died that year,

Michael who lived in the next house down who was a little pigeon-toed and was my friend until at school other kids started making fun of me and then he wasn't, and Jenny who used to stand at the bus stop, hip cocked out and foot turned out like a ballet dancer, and who later became an artist. My mom and dad's best friends lived in the next house over, and we called them Aunty Sadhana and Uncle Satish. They had two sons who I used to babysit on Friday nights when our parents went out. We played games, or they colored while I watched Dallas, put them to bed, and then watched Falcon Crest.

Even though Uncle Satish was a tennis player and very healthy, he had a heart attack one year and died. Aunty Sadhana and the boys moved away to California. Years later when I was in San Jose I met up with them for dinner. We were reminiscing about the old days, and Sadhana said, with feeling, "Those were my golden years. Those were the best years of my life."

The younger son burst out laughing, and said, with Satish's voice, "How can you say that, mom?! That was twenty years ago!" And Aunty Sadhana started laughing too, looking down at her salad plate, laughing until tears came to her eyes.

I was cruising down the street, very, very slowly, looking at each house as I passed. Would the people in the houses see me? What would they think I was doing? Could I stop and tell them the stories of the people who lived in their houses? As I cruised toward the Oberoi house, whose kids I also used to babysit, I marveled that the house looked so beautiful—there had been a fire there and the

Oberois had to stay in a hotel while it was being refurbished.

But before I reached that house that had once been on fire I passed the house where a boy named Jason lived, who in junior high before his voice changed always sang the national anthem at all the school assemblies in his trembling soprano. In high school he hung himself and died. I still remember hearing the announcement at school and wondering if his younger sister was in school that day. Where was Stacey now? Where were his parents? As I wondered, a woman came out of the house toward the curb to bring in the trash bin and the recycling bin. She had short blond hair cut beautifully, and a big friendly smile.

Should I tell her? Could I? Would she want to know that a boy died in her house? Would she rather not know? Did the real estate agent tell her? Did she sometimes pass the bedroom on her way downstairs and wonder about history and all the ways we touch each other? Does something still hang in the air?

She caught my gaze through the window looking and she waved, smiling at me the way you smile at someone you know. I smiled back, waving my hand, not just holding it up the way you wave at someone you don't know, motionless, half way between a wave and a salute, but rather shaking the hand as I waved, the way you wave to someone you know well, someone you have only recently parted from.

She grabbed the handle on the trash bin and I cruised on, and that was the nothing that passed between us.

Sajjad Ali

The single appearance of my grandfather Sajjad Ali in the public print archive of Canada is in a captioned photograph about his death, which appeared in the July 11, 1980 edition of the Winnipeg Free Press. Neither the man himself nor his name as I knew it appears.

He is identified as "Mohammed Sayeed," his legal name but not the one his family knew him by. He appears in the photograph as a body lying in the street, covered by a white sheet. For the first time I see the name of the man who killed him, the driver of the pickup, Allan John Dmytruk, age 35, of Setter Street.

Is he the same Allan John Dmytruk, who on October 23, 1968 at the age of 23 was convicted of armed robbery as reported by the same Winnipeg Free Press? It seems likely. And is he still alive? It feels important to me to know.

"I learned the name of the man who killed my grandfather," I write to a friend.

The man who killed my grandfather. I had never written that phrase before, never thought of it that way. He died. It was an accident. We lost him. But there had been a man driving that truck, who wasn't looking. A man with a life of his own that went on, though I don't know in what fashion.

My grandfather lay in the road, two policemen standing over him. He is veiled from view, covered by the sheet. His name looks unfamiliar to me, and the address given was not where he actually lived, but the address of his daughter and son-in-law around the corner.

He was a ghost in the history of Canada, unseen, unnamed, without location.

The Flight of the Icarus

For our final project in high school Physics class we had to use only toothpicks and glue to build a structure around an egg that would protect it from being broken after being dropped from a second floor balcony onto the thinly carpeted floor of the auditorium, the same auditorium in which the Drama Club would later practice our production of Our Town in which I had been cast as Si Crowell, not a very important role, only six lines in the second act, a single scene, but enough to keep away from home for another two hours at the end of the school day.

The director decided to use all of the cast members with few lines as extras in the wedding scene and we were supposed to enter, find another cast member, and make brief improvised small talk over the music that would be playing as we took our seats in the pantomimed church.

My friend Beth—who was also my girlfriend, back when I imagined I wanted girlfriends—and I decided that our exchange would consist of me greeting her with a big cheerful smile, saying, "Fuck you, Erna," to which she would reply with equal pleasure, "Fuck you, Si."

Small stage time aside, Si Crowell is actually considered by critics to be a somewhat important character in the play—he is meant to symbolize the passing of time, and a foreshadow to the deaths in the third act, his older brother Joe having had the paper route in Act 1 and having been killed, by Act 2, in the Great War.

If there was any character in Our Town I actually did identify with, it was Simon Stimson, the drunk choir director, who cannot abide the pettinesses and limitations of small town life. By Act 3, he too is dead, implied to be by his own hand. Bryan, the kid who played Simon with a little too much realistic flair, was the most beautiful and melancholy boy in school. He spent most of his time hanging around the art wing, and in all the years that have followed, I never heard about him again, though I dream he escaped the suburbs and climbed a mountain and lives among clouds.

As one of the ghosts in the cemetery says, "If it t'aint rain, it's a three day blow."

There was something thrilling, I don't have to tell you, about saying "Fuck you" on a stage, in a period play, in front of an audience of hundreds of students and teachers, including Vice Principal Sugg, who always vetted every play the Drama Club wanted to mount, to make sure it was appropriate for high school audiences, and in a different way, more secret, more ridiculous, to say "If it tain't rain, it's a three day blow."

I was bullied almost every day in high school, either for being Muslim or for being gay, which I didn't even know myself then. I was so good at hiding it that not even my best friends knew.

Still, physics and loneliness somehow got me through.

Rather than create some kind of logical armature to cup the egg or to successively break its fall in careful stages, I just started at the shell, adding a thicket of toothpicks at every angle, building outward in a clustered mess. I called my ship the Icarus and everyone teased me and jeered at how foolish it was, that it would never survive the fall, little ball of thorns that it was.

Mr. Schumacher's face betrayed nothing as he carried the little crown of thorns holding its fragile heart up to the balcony. He held it over the railing like something sacred and looked down at me, a question in his eyes.

I didn't see the moment he let it go, it just seemed to be traveling toward me, the wooden shards built so tightly around it, I wouldn't have guessed there was anything within.

The carpet at the bottom had already been covered with a white plastic tarp, now thick with sticky white albumen and slick with yellow streaks of yolk. There was no sound as the vessel landed other than a soft crumpling as some of the tips gave way. Mr. Tuzzolino, who was waiting at the bottom, bent over to pick up the mostly intact structure. "Do you see how hardly any of it is broken?" he asked the class, holding it out to show them. "Because of all the different angles, each toothpick reinforces every other."

I couldn't explain to you how I knew what to do. My math was terrible and I was on track to fail the class, not least of which was because my lab partner Felipe—a foreign exchange student from Venezuela with slender thighs and a long sweeping mullet that fell across his lithe neck like feathers and who used to weigh himself every day after lunch, which he skipped in order to run endless laps around the indoor track, logging his weight in precise numbers in the back of his Physics notebook week by week (63.5 kg, 62 kg, 60.7 kg, 59.4 kg)—was at least as dumb as I was and definitely as bad at math.

Even though I desperately wanted to be an ACTOR I am pretty sure the only reason I was cast as Si Crowell was because Nilay Shah, a 4-and-a-half foot tall, 95 lb freshman who was a five-alarm charmer, had been cast as Joe, even though Nilay was Jain and we were Muslim—really Muslim, so Muslim we had a giant framed picture of Khomeini above our fireplace where most kids had a family picture or a sculpture of birds or a vase of flowers—and everyone always lumped us together.

As it was, my egg was one of only three in the entire class that didn't break and Mr. Schumacher, well aware that I knew nothing about centripetal or centrifugal force, nor velocity or matter or mass nor bodies at motion or rest, still determined that my feat of somehow surviving gravity merited at the very least a B+.

Translating the Gayatri Mantra in Varkala

"We meditate on that most adored Supreme Lord, the creator, whose divine light illumines all realms. May this divine light illumine our intellect."

—*Sri Sathya Sai Baba*

Om: OM, the primeval sound;

Bhur: the physical body/physical realm;

Bhuvah: the life force/the mental realm;

Svah: the soul/spiritual realm;

Tat: That (God);

Savitur: the Sun, Creator (source of all life);

Vareñyam: adore;

Bhargo: effulgence (divine light);

Devasya: supreme Lord;

Dhīmahi: meditate;

Dhiyo: the intellect;

Yo: May this light;

Nah: our;

Pracodayāt: illumine/inspire.

In the yoga class on the rooftop of the Baby Hotel we chant the Gayatri Mantra:

> *om bhūr bhuvaḥ svaḥ*
> *tat savitur vareṇyaṃ*
> *bhargo devasya dhīmahi*
> *dhiyo yo naḥ pracodayāt*

Primeval sound the earth this mind in breath
Source that the sun adore and is adored
Bright Lord measure me
Inside the spark eternal I resound

22

On the street after the class, mats rolled up under our arms, the students gather and talk before we part. The teacher says: Come back next time without eating in the morning and you will achieve Crow.

I waggle my head side to side.

How to explain what that most Indian of gestures means? Neither yes nor no, more "It will happen as it happens."

The streets of Varkala run along a cliff overlooking the Arabian Sea.

Far from home I found a home or is it that I have no home?

OM this world in space boundless ,
Profound stellar orb ablaze
Remove the darkness shine shine
I linger in this opening

On the solstice I float in my body like a compass needle.

The men here are limp, they touch each others' backs, kiss each others' mouths.

So what am I if not a man?

The woman in the store around the corner from my house means well when she takes stock of my hair, my eyes, my clothes and mouth and calls me "ma'am."

My mother asks will I be home next holiday and I say "inshallah."

How to explain what that most Muslim of expressions means? Not yes or no but "as God wills."

And there lies the difference between the sun that shines and the moon that is shone upon, the difference between the genders in my body, the difference between a lifetime and a life:

is God a willful actor or a phenomenon engendered by infinite choices by infinite humans?

Sound	• this-body	• a Realm
that-which-IS	• solar	• flares
Lucent	• called	• here
who-I-AM	• shown	• now/ in/ spire

Prayer Rug

Given to me as a gift when I was a child, I learned from it that you always take God with you.

Folded around objects: beads on a string, a tablet of clay from Karbala, a small book of prayers.

Being told once by a younger Muslim writer, "you paved a way for us" is still no comfort for this loneliness.

I learned all my prayers by transliteration.

Patterns in the rug: how do you read them?

Carried easily around the world though meant at sunrise, noon, midafternoon, sunset and night to draw one back to a single point on the planet.

Road of woven silk, who travels ahead of me paving the way.

My body is my prayer rug, my spine beads on a string, inside my mouth is that book, the one I am writing.

And what of all the unanswered letters, those forgotten on the way, like George, a lonely older man I knew long ago in my twenties. He would pick me up from the gym and take me back to his house and give me long massages.

Those prayer rugs from all the epic stories that can bear you up into the sky, across the city landscape, singing.

When I think of what it means to pray, I remember George saying with forlorn gratitude as his hands moved down my body, "Thank you for letting me touch you."

Afterward, I would sit in George's tub and he would give me a bucket-bath, the way my father did, pouring water over my head at the end.

When I try to remember my first prayer rug, in my mind is that red and gold silken janamaaz, but on my skin I feel George engulfing me after the bath with a huge towel, rubbing me vigorously to dry my skin and hair.

Graffiti

One of the towns I used to live in was called Beacon, so named for Mount Beacon, not really a mountain but a hill over the Hudson where the revolutionaries had placed a beacon so they could warn towns upriver if the British breached New York—the first in a series of signal fires in a chain running north of the city to Albany.

We used to hike up the slopes, passing the great fallen cables of what had once been a funicular running to the top, where there had been a hotel and casino, both burned in a fire. As you climbed, you would see hawks floating level with you on the updraft and looking out past the town, see the river turning and eddying at what locals called "World's End," the place the estuary waters of the Atlantic turned and returned.

One day we decided that we would stay along the fallen cables and climb all the way up to the top to see if we could find the place the hotel once stood, but nothing was up there but the ruined funicular house, its brick walls long since crumbled, the spools open to the sky. The forest had long since covered over any ruin there might have been.

I feel something of that in my own life: any ruin of the past, any conflagration, covered eventually by the forest of time: days and years that accrete with new lives. But what is left in the woods can still blaze alive to kill us.

Once I was walking with my parents along the bike path near their suburban home in Western New York. We had a hard time with ordinary conversation, even small talk, because there was so much I could not bring myself to say, so much they did not want to hear. But walking on the path was one thing we could do. An hour stroll before dinner each day when I visited, this was after my father's heart attack which required a regular light exercise routine, but before my mother's stroke had impacted her memory a little and made her substantially more chatty.

This time it was me who kept up a running commentary, noticing the plants in the ditch along the trail, pointing out a bird in the sky, saying hello to people coming the other way. I was running out of topics, my mind turning toward the things I held inside, the things I would never say, and then ahead, maybe twenty feet, in giant letters stretching across the black asphalt in white letters someone had spray-painted "GOD IS GAY."

Even the stone wanted me to speak.

Yet on Mount Beacon, when we walked inside the four broken walls, we saw in coils of blue and white paint carefully calligraphed across the ruined south wall, "ALL FAGS MUST DIE."

My mind wonders back across the broken wheels, and iron cables lying limply down through the forest, and I think, it's true, we all must. Each body is a stack of twigs, corded together and already combusting.

And then I think: who is the person who chose to hike strenuously two miles up in the late summer to a broken house on the bald summit to write these words.

And do they ever return, repeating the hike, to confront and consult the public marks of their secret hate, to read it aloud, to see the granular syllables of color again coalesce with a hiss on the surface of stone.

plays

Going Out

Characters:

Maggie, a 40-something year old woman

Scene:

The kitchen of Maggie's apartment, a counter with high chairs with their backs to the audience. The fridge is stage right; door is next to the fridge. Bedroom is off stage left.

Maggie enters from bedroom. She has a canvas tote bag carried in the crook of her elbow. She opens a cupboard and takes out a bottle of gin and put it in her bag. She crosses to the fridge. She opens the fridge and puts a bottle of tonic water in her bag. She pulls out a lime. She pauses. She considers. She hangs the bag on the back of a chair and gets out a tumbler and puts ice cubes in the tumbler. She gets a small knife and positions the lime to cut a wedge then stops. Considers. Shakes her head. She puts away the knife and dumps the ice in the sink. She puts the gin and the tonic water back into the fridge. She picks up the bag and takes her keys out. She pauses in front of the door. She turns back and fetches knife, lime, glass. Takes a ceramic to-go coffee cup from the cupboard and mixes a gin and tonic in it. Cuts the lime and drops some pieces in. Replaces the tonic and the gin. Goes toward the door. Stops. Goes back to the cupboard and gets the gin and puts it in her tote. Balancing with her keys in one hand and the to-go cup in the other, she prepares to head out.

MAGGIE: (speaking to herself)
You'll be fine. You'll be fine. You're not a drunk. You're just having a really bad year.

Maggie exits.

Explaining

Characters:

Raj, a gay man, aged 50-65, trim and very well groomed and dressed.

Ben, a visibly much younger gay man, perhaps aged 25-30.

A waiter.

Scene:

A patio of a bar. Ben and Raj are leaning on the balcony. It appears they know each other and have been talking for some time. Ben has probably just asked Raj a question as the play begins. Pleasant music is playing. A waiter may walk by with a drink order or bring an order to the men during the play. Throughout the play only Raj speaks, with such pauses as feel natural. Ben reacts. The director and actor can determine in performance what Ben's body language and reactions will be.

RAJ:

I had a son. He died. When something like that happens, you don't understand. You think you're the one who shouldn't be alive anymore. But you go on. You live because everyone thinks you're supposed to. You live because your body doesn't know what else to do. You have another child. She needs you. She doesn't know what to do either. It feels wrong. Your son is dead and you're still alive. You bargain. You may even plan. To not be alive anymore either. How you would do it. What you have to take care of first. Every day it feels like your heart breaks one more time. And then you go on. You think somehow that your heart will never stop breaking. And then you live. And one day you wake up, you make coffee. Out of the blue it occurs to you, you know, you suddenly think that your heart will never break again. Then it breaks again.

Idaho

Characters:

Neel, a young man, in the range of 20s-30s.

Bartender

Patrons

Scene:

Neel is sitting at a bar. His back is to the audience. The bartender is serving people at the bar. There are people sitting on either side of him, talking to each other. He is talking to whoever will listen, sometimes the bartender, sometimes to the people on either side of him, but no one is really listening to him. He is probably not aware of this, or if he becomes aware of this it doesn't stop him. Neel may or may not be drinking as he talks. He may or may not become tipsy or drunk as he talks.

NEEL:

Idaho weather doesn't give a shit about you. Idaho weather is not fucking interested in your nonsense. It blows your umbrella out but what are you supposed to do? There's nowhere else to go, the hotel coffee is crap and you're down to your last two Xanax.

Anyhow, so my sister stopped talking to me yesterday. How do I know she "stopped"? I mean, it's only been a day, but something about the conversation felt final. It happens. I'm not really sure if I'll hear from her again next week, next month or next year but I know it won't be until I decide to write to her or until I go home to visit my folks and just kind of run into her and she will act like nothing is different, nothing has changed and anyhow the last time I saw her, she barely said hello, she sat at the table near the door, didn't even come over to say hi, just played Candy Crush on her phone for a couple hours until the kids were ready to leave.

I don't know. Boise. What a place. Today I had the shittiest sushi I've ever had this side of the Rockies. Sure, sushi in Idaho is automatically questionable but I'm vegan so you know I thought I was home free.

I went to a party last night and there was another vegan there! I joked with him, I said we're the only two vegans in the entire state of Idaho and he laughed. Then the appetizers came out and there was a big plate of chicken wings, which—I'm from Buffalo so of course I want the wings—they looked so good. And this kid—the other vegan—just starts dogging them. And he's finished about three, putting the bones back on the plate, and I'm staring at him and he finally sees me staring at him, so he finishes eating the fourth wing and drags a forearm across his mouth to clean up the grease and he says, "I'm a vegan but I still eat wings."

Anyhow, I finish the sushi and I'm just sitting there and one table over is probably the most beautiful man I've ever seen. He has salt and pepper dreadlocks that are tied back with pink and purple ribbons, which ordinarily I would think was a questionable choice, but I'm willing to forgive him anything on account of those eyes. Not grey, not blue, something weirdly in between? Contacts? No. He's huddled up with two other people—an older woman in a black sweatshirt, nice smile, a younger woman who is skinny in way that seems like maybe it's dangerous. Like she needs a sandwich. Their conversation, the little I can hear without seeming too obvious about the fact that I'm listening, hovers halfway between Christian ministry, some business self help and more or less generic Chicken Soup for the Soul kind of shit.

And it's still raining. And that wind. Someone told me last week that they knew a person who was loading groceries into their car at the supermarket when the wind blew the car door closed on them and broke their leg. Broke. Their. Leg. I mean, what even is that?

The people at the next table are talking about who knows what the Final Judge (my beautiful dreadlocked friend's term) will say about all of this, probably nothing. Hey, did you know that in Idaho it is a felony to not disclose your HIV status to a potential sexual partner? True fact.

Then get this: the most beautiful man in the world (so far) stands up with his friends to leave and it turns out that even though he has a normal sized head and big shoulders, he is the shortest one in the group by a foot. He wouldn't come up to my elbow. He's Tyrion-sized. It somehow makes him hotter.

You know, I really want to say I don't care, I'm used to loneliness, that I don't need the sun, that I'm in the West now where the ground is cold, and the air is ferocious.

In the West the wind can kill you. Sisters don't call. The content of your blood can make you criminal. In the West, even vegans eat meat.

poems

The Museum of Flight

All boys secretly want to fall
sent like thunder westward

Sense-sure and censured they twist
out of the wings fastened to their backs

Itching always for more blue
suspended endlessly in the moment of fall

Here in the sky ward
you can count them:

Panicked or resigned,
all heading in the blue direction,

Their fathers always at a loss for words.

Here is the disobedient one who was
lightning-struck

The stupid one who lost control of the horses

Here is the one seized by his heel and hurled down

And here the wild one who flew straight for the sun

Here the frightened one who stowed away
on the silver boat bound for the storm.

They all raced away from rules like sea-drunk criminals
hopelessly confused about the laws of men and gods

Caught by gravity, hurtling like bolts of silk
unrolling across the sky

Going on and on about infinity and eternity
the whole way down.

Dispersal

Water seeps in through the foundation
of the house

Apple branches cut and brought inside
From the late winter afternoon and forced to bloom

What's left on the lake bed to harvest
And clarify

I take attendance of myself
Half absent and drifting

Michael Burkard? Present.
Jean Valentine? Present.

Fox Week

Two wounded foxes linger in the yard for
a week.

Only once in my life have I ever asked to be
answered.

But this time I am a fox in the yard who needs
no answer.

I remember nothing of how I was wounded so I
must be at home.

In-Flight Movie

In a place real not real
White space beneath

We tear from the ground
To race earth's turn

Stay ahead of dusk
On the way home from home

Flying west in the last light
Sad as a cinder, I weep like a stone

Zephyr

The child astronomer hides trembling at school
From the other boys wanting only to

Unfold himself in every way imaginable
beautifully sky-drunk beneath the pine trees

At night he plots the location of the constellation Zephyr
imagining the cruelest boy of all wearing its shirt of stars

Evenings he leaves his windows open
so the hot spring wind can slide warmly in

Falcon

His life then lifted
Just for a moment then
Plummeted down

Sky to beach,
white wings unfurl
Useless but beautiful

Bird of dust thrust landward
And learn through life in the body
Of a man

what it means
To be flawed
A follower fallen

His brother the falcon flew

On a silver boat chasing the storm

While he stayed dumbly home

The Year of Autumn

The orchestra of oncoming rain tunes its note
to the sound of a spider descending from the beam,

Perfect me then in dissonance,
Late summer's tumescence, surge against my skin,

A dissident thrusting himself between the bars
of sonorous afternoon, aiming for his escape

Who was it that first hears the thunder crack
like a child hiding in a cello case, reciting Dickinson,

that sends us scurrying for the upper floors
to close all the windows, unplug appliances,

Bit by bit in the earth disappearing I am
shirking every chore wanting only to transcribe

the storm's randy tune, I split for the storm-licked grass
while the wind outside reveals the wind inside.

I hold the encroaching chill off with one stiff arm
while September in hot slicks comes over me—

Slipknot

I want to crucify my injuries through which I know

God that weirdly pronounced word is not what
    I mean when

Silent among species we make ourselves strangers

By among the infinity of matter tracing a tentative
    body's shape

And with sight tricked by time pronounce in the
    radiant season a name

Lighthouse

Shining over the harbor
Lonely and unchurched

Interrupting the southern sky
When in the dark

We built our way by current
And star

To fathom is the ruin
Of dusk and depth

acknowledgments

"Sweet Nothing" appeared in *Mississippi Review*.
"Translating the Gayatri Mantra" appeared in *The Georgia Review*.

The poems appeared in a limited edition chapbook called "Hello My Name Is _____ ," published by Foundlings Press.

about the author

Kazim Ali writes in, across, through, and against multiple genres, including poetry, essay, memoir, fiction, journalism, translation, and the genre-queer. A former yoga teacher, lobbyist, and grass roots organizer, he currently lives in the traditional lands of the Kumeyaay people, where he chairs the Department of Literature at the University of California, San Diego.